“Original humor.
forget. B
Ke

“Very funny, wond
has looked at the game of golf in quite this way. Truly an original – can’t wait for more!”
John J. Glozek, Jr., Publisher, *Long Island Golfer*

“DeVere’s stories are interesting to me in a way quite rare: They are warm-hearted, intelligent and funny. He clearly knows his stuff about golf.”
George Fuller, Managing Editor, *Links Magazine*

“This is the S.J. Pearlman of the 1990s, with dashes of Twain and James Thurber thrown in for good measure. But the style is all his own. From the first story, it’s obvious deVere takes the humor of golf very seriously. Bravo!”
Terry Bunton, golf writer, novelist

“DeVere brings it all back down to earth in *I Golf, Therefore I Am*. Funny, funny writing for a funny, funny game.”
William Price Fox, *Dr. Golf*

“Many of the situations and characters ring so true to life, I find myself looking at my students from deVere’s point of view ... a very dangerous situation. Thoroughly enjoyable reading.”
Don Trahan, PGA Master Professional

“Hard to believe but true. ... I’m still laughing!”
Bob Thomas, PGA Professional

“DeVere makes me laugh. As a neglected ‘golf widow,’ *I Golf, Therefore I Am* has given me insights into how to cope with someone who spends an entire afternoon of his life participating in a very questionable sport. Four stars, or whatever they might say in golf!”
Sarah Gilbert, *Hairdo, Dixie Riggs*

I Golf, Therefore I Am
(frustrated & humble . . . but hopeful)

Saron Press, Ltd. / January 1996
Box 4990, Hilton Head Island, SC 29938

Printed in the United States of America
Streeter Printing and Graphics, Inc., Augusta, Georgia

Library of Congress Catalog Card Number: 95-73105
ISBN 0-9650791-0-4

I ~~Think~~ Golf, Therefore I Am

(frustrated & humble ... but hopeful)

VOLUME ONE

— ~~DESCARTES~~ Devere

Paul deVere
Illustrated by Ashley Holt
Edited by Lewis Hammet

SARON PRESS, LTD.
HILTON HEAD ISLAND, SOUTH CAROLINA

Dedication & Acknowledgments

To my father, who did not play the game but helped me develop a sense of humor about the impossible; to my mother, who unknowingly encouraged what some have called my rather odd (I prefer fresh) way of looking at impossible situations; to my beautiful, beloved wife, my inspiration and favorite golf partner; to Sarah and Aaron, my beautiful, beloved children and further inspirations; to Ann, Marty and Dan, with love; to Don, my pro and friend; to Bob, my friend and pro; to the Hilton Head Island golf professionals for allowing me to wander their rough; to all my friends at Hyatt Resorts – a class act, golf becomes you; to my fellow golf writers, who continue to lend me stories and put up with my game; to Arch, Marshall and Liz for extraordinary patience; to Fathers Dan and Don; to dear friends Tim, Michael, Jim and George, who, in their own way, made this happen; to my valiant and trustworthy editor, Lewis Hammet, who *really* made this happen; and finally, to my faithful readers, who kept telling me I ought to do this book. Thank you.

Editor's Note: The stories contained within this volume represent a choice collection of the syndicated column, "Me & My Pro" (formerly "From the Tips"), by author and golfer Paul deVere. First published in *Hilton Head Monthly* magazine, the following tales of the apprentice and his guide are now read by amateur and professional golfers throughout the United States, as evidenced by a blanket increase in the nation's mean golf score.

Contents

Introduction

When I first took up the game, two events left indelible marks upon my golfing soul that caused me to write and play. First, because I honestly believed you could learn something from books, I went in search of a written guide that would help the beginning golfer. The few I found were confusing, contradictory, filled with intimidating golf jargon, and they all lacked humor. Thus challenged, I decided I would write a beginners' tome myself and set about seeking the gurus of the game to give me expert advice. By the fourth guru, I knew I was on to something.

My discovery was that beginners didn't need yet another confusing, contradictory, intimidating, humorless manual (now available at your favorite book store). They needed a way to deal with an impossible game. They didn't need someone to tell them how to hit it off the first tee. They needed someone to tell them how to find the first tee.

Golf may be the only sport in the world where you not only can locate golf titles in the sports section of Walden Books, you can also find them in the self-help *(Putt Your Way to CEO)*, philosophy *(God, Golf & The Big Bang)*, alternative medicine *(Acupuncture Can Add Ten Yards)* and paranormal psychology *(Be the Tee, Be the Ball)* sections. Nevertheless, in my search through the hundreds of instructional videos and golf magazines, I found nothing to help a 40-plus-year-old person determine which club should go where in the golf bag or how to deduct greens fees from your tax return without triggering an audit. No master ever defined "bag drop" for me. Not one touring pro ever wrote a word about the proper stance when shelling out hundreds of dollars at the pro shop counter (and that's just for range balls). You can learn how to swing in 25 different languages, but where do you find it written that, in many instances, the key to the comfort station (i.e., toilet) out on the course is on your golf cart's key ring? Given the appropriate circumstance, which is more important?

In an attempt to fill this obvious and significant void, I began to write these little missives called "From the Tips," later renamed "Me & My Pro." For the thousands of cards and letters of gratitude my fellow sojourners have sent me, I offer my humble thanks. For the lawsuits my innocent suggestions may have spurred, I say, "Good luck."

Indelible mark one.

The second indelible mark had to do with my first official golf lesson. It was with my brother-in-law, a true, blue PGA professional. After 45 minutes on the fundamentals (actually, it should be "fundamental" since I hadn't been able to learn the proper grip during that time), he suggested, in a very kind way, it would be best if I continued playing tennis.

Difficult to hit that little ball with my racquet, I said jokingly.

He jokingly went back to teaching me the proper grip for the next two hours. His tears, I knew, were tears of joy.

Yet his funny little comment had triggered something in me – an epiphany, if you will. From that moment on, I began to see the inherent humor of the game. I also began to see the golf professional as a compassionate, wise and very patient person who overcomes the greatest of obstacles (golfers) and the totally inconsiderate (golfers) in order to help us (golfers) enjoy this delightful game (golf).

To the ladies and gentlemen of this select fraternity, may the following help you get through the night.

Paul deVere
Hilton Head Island, South Carolina
January 1996

Ever Notice Golf and God Both Start With G?

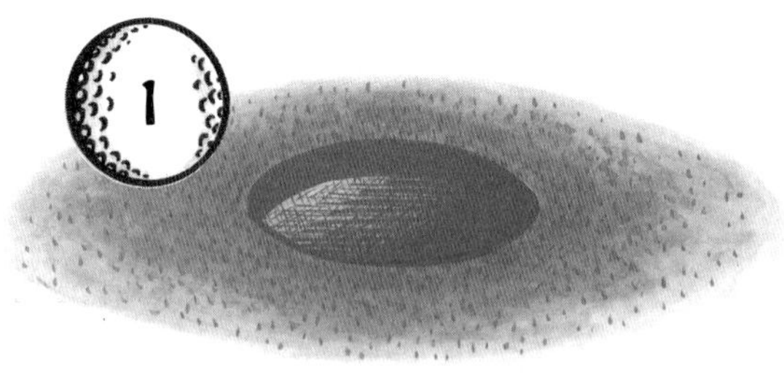

There may be no other sport so linked to theology than golf. No disrespect or sacrilege is meant with this statement, although I have always believed, since my tenure as an altar boy back at St. Martin de Tours, that God had a terrific sense of humor. When I took up the game later in life, I discovered that this omniscient humor is no more manifest than in the game of golf. While Scottish shepherds (related to Jewish shepherds?) may be credited with the game's beginnings, it took a much higher form of intelligence (and wit) to create such a diversion.

On the links, as in life, the player is responsible for his or her own actions. A serious slice is not caused by the luck of the draw, but by our own personal inability to follow the straight and narrow. The nuns taught us that life's dilemmas were tests of our self-control. What greater test of self-control than teeing up your third ball after dumping two drives into the little pond in front of the tee, supposedly out of play?

Is it not Heaven on earth when a high handicapper shoots 10 strokes below his or her average score? Or pure Hell when a low handicapper lips out on No. 18 to lose the tour-

nament by one stroke? I was trying to explain this to my pro recently. He seemed a good deal less than impressed.

"You might be overdoing it a bit," he suggested as we approached the tee box on the next hole.

Overdo? Think of the greens, I said. More prayers are said over six-foot putts than in any church. I mentioned that I had seen even his lips move as he'd appealed to a higher authority to help him sink his three-footer on the last green.

This new theory of mine (I am nothing if not a theoretical golfer – my wife would say "a golfer in theory") excited me.

As I stepped up to the ball, I pictured myself as a valiant Crusader in quest of the Holy Grail. I noticed where my ball landed and pictured myself as an early Christian martyr being thrown into a pit of vipers.

"I'll help you find it," my pro offered. "Maybe it hit a tree."

God's will, I said as we entered the evil domain. Indeed, it reminded me of the Garden of Eden after the Fall.

"Watch out for snakes," my pro cautioned as we tramped further into the forest. A few minutes later, he found it. There it was, my lost sheep waiting to be saved.

Then I heard myself beseech the Almighty to damn the ball, my driver and myself, and darkness came over the land.

"Just pitch it out," my pro suggested, "I think it's going to rain."

We finished the hole, but due to the lightning and thunder and sheets of rain, we could not finish the game. Safely seated in the clubhouse grill and quaffing down a mug of my favorite dark ale, I watched my pro add up the scorecard. Him keeping my score was part of my training since I suffered from the golfer's common affliction of counting sixes and sevens but writing down fours.

His eyes lit up. "I'll be darned," he said. "Even though you were falling apart those last few holes, you were shooting your best game ever. I guess we'll never know."

Best ever? Really? I was beside myself with joy. I thought of all the sensational stories I could tell, all beginning with, "If it weren't for the rain ..."

Truly, I concluded, there is a God. ■

New Year's Revolutions

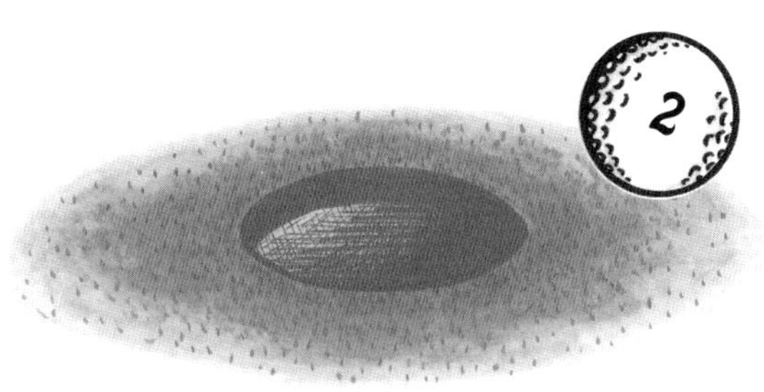

'Twas three days before Christmas and all through the house, not a present was present, not even for my wife.

I had purchased one of those buy-three-get-one-free boxes of balls for her in early November but, due to a couple of unexpected games I became involved in prior to Christmas, they had disappeared into lagoons and thick vegetation. I had also gone through most of the balls I'd purchased for my six-year-old twins. Ever since their first Christmas, I have stuffed at least one sleeve of my favorite golf balls into their stockings. Following my rules for enlightened parenting, I felt this was an ideal way to demonstrate the virtue of sharing with their father.

At 72 hours before "C-Day" I was, as they say, somewhat short of the green. So I did what I've been doing for years. I made panic calls to every editor with whom I had an assignment and promised that I would actually meet my deadline if they could front me a few bucks.

As I pushed my empty cart along the isles of Wal-Mart on Christmas Eve (they were putting out the Easter baskets), my wallet bulging with my payment-in-advance wealth, I was unable to find one item on the kids' wish list. I started to make my New Year's Revolutions then and there.

This is not a misprint. Most people can and do make well-meaning, earnest, thoughtful "resolutions" for the New Year. However, I have learned that, no matter what economic circumstance a golfer finds him- or herself in, changing the course of one's life requires something much stronger. That is, nothing short of a revolution.

For example, no matter how paralyzed with desire you are to go with the group to Pinehurst for a couple of days, if the kids' birthday falls on one of those days, you can't go. Period. Similarly, if your significant other's birthday happens to be one of those days, you must at least fax or phone your good wishes. Be a revolutionary!

Next, try these equations. Mortgage payment equals secure shelter for your family for another month. New driver equals the amount of your mortgage payment but promises 10 more yards. Revolt! Pay the mortgage! (If, however, you can actually get 10 more yards with the driver, you are in what ethicists call a conundrum, which, ethically, calls for a flip of the coin.)

This year, vow – on the Bible, Mao's little Red Book (or Harvey's), the Deceleration of Independence and Magna Charta – that three-putting will NOT cause you to torment your putter, the ball, members of your foursome, your family or your family's dog. Take a stand!

Finally, and without equivocation, make every effort to learn to count. Some folks I play with have a tough time here. See if you can pass this simple test. One off the tee and into the trees. Two out of the trees onto the fairway. One into the sand bunker, two out onto the green. Three putts and you're in the hole. Score? If your answer is five or lower, learning to count should be your first New Year's Revolution.

Mine was to leave the Christmas money in the savings account, no matter how reasonable the greens fees might seem in the off season. My second

Henceforth: I will make every effort to remove my golf socks from my golf shoes the moment I get home.

was inspired by my bride. Henceforth: I will make every effort to remove my golf socks from my golf shoes the moment I get home. After a three-week hiatus from the game, I removed the still-damp socks from my shoes in the presence of my wife.

"My God, how revolting!" she gasped in that funny way of hers.

Filled with defiance, I marched to the trashcan and took the first step toward galvanizing my radical new series of revolutionary measures.

I dropped them in. ■

The Touron Factor

I have the privilege, pleasure and responsibility of living in a part of this great nation where well in excess of one million of my fellow human beings of all races, nationalities, creeds, occupations, etc., vacation annually.

Those in the tourism industry call them "visitors" or "guests," although there are a few politically incorrect residents of this lush, semi-tropical island who still refer to them as "TOURISTS" (i.e., "Totally Onerous, Ungrateful, Rotten, Insensitive, Supercilious ToadS).

On the golf course, I have heard some usually mild-mannered, even-tempered golf professionals identify certain members of this million-plus hoard as "Tourons," a creative combining of tourist and the "M" word (rhymes with Boron). The title is almost always followed by an exclamation point or preceded by the Creator's common name coupled with a word that rhymes with "Spam."

Of course, when I first heard these purveyors of good sportsmanship and impeccable manners use such language, I was shocked. Granted, when these "visitors" and "guests" jam our local boulevards, causing my older car to overheat, I often

question their parentage, intellectual capacity and associate them with one particular part of their anatomy. But on the golf course – one of the last bastions of decorum? By golf professionals? How else would these pros make their living if it wasn't for the tourons ... er, ... visitors?

I mentioned this to my pro just moments before my wife and I were ready to tee off. My pro, generous to a fault, had arranged a tee time for me within minutes of my calling and hinting that *"It-was-my-birthday-and-the-kids-were-at-school-and-I-have-to-play-now-pleeeeeeease!"*

"It happens in the heat of the moment," my pro explained, his face clouding with painful memories. "It happens when they run their carts up onto the green or into a lagoon. When the two-balls-off-the-first-tee tradition turns into six balls off the first, five off the second, four off the third. It happens when they take a wrong turn and end up playing the same hole twice. It happens when the ranger asks if they mind letting a foursome play through and they ask what 'play through' means. It happens when they lay down in the fairway, when they leave sand bunkers looking like battlefields."

I understand, I said quietly, trying to soothe him.

My pro, my wife and I waited quietly for the group ahead of us to tee off. Judging from their outfits and the way their cart was parked diagonally across the path, I guessed they were "visitors."

"In fact, most of them are good people," my pro continued. "They've worked an entire year, often at a job they don't particularly love, to afford a week away from the burden of their daily responsibilities. They deserve a good time. And they have chosen to have it here. That's a real compliment to us. But some of them seem to leave their brain on the dining-room table when they go on vacation."

The foursome was ready to tee off. A mighty swing by the first player hurled the ball far right into the trees. The second rocketed it just past the ladies' tee. The third and fourth went deep left. I was becoming impatient. The children would be in grad school by the time we finished this round.

My pro ambled up to the tee, shook hands with the players and said something I couldn't hear. They all smiled. He ambled back over to our cart.

"You can play though," he said, his hand resting on the cart.

How'd you do it? I asked.

"I told them you were a tourist and they would be safer if you were in front of them."

My pro has class. ■

Hosel-free Golf

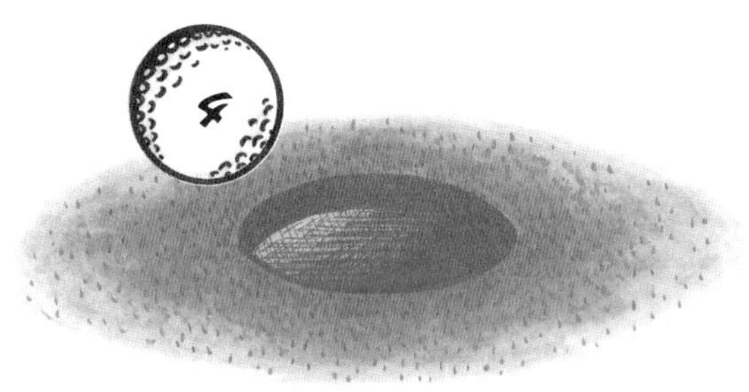

My pro and I were out on the driving range. I was learning why my ball was going further right than a South American dictator. We normally don't spend too much time on the driving range, but I was scheduled to play the following day with relatives who all shot in the low 80s, and I didn't want my humiliation to begin until we were closer to the green.

I like the driving range because it's wide and you don't have to find your balls. I asked my pro why we didn't spend more time here.

"Most courses have about four par fives," he explained. "You play from the white tees. You probably only use your driver four times in a game." He also explained that that was why we spent more time on the iron range, the pitching range, the chipping range and the putting range.

We discovered I was coming across the ball with the face of my driver open. Being a left-handed control freak (I swing right-handed), my left hand was not allowing my right hand to square the club up as God intended.

We adjusted, and I smacked one reasonably straight. I knew I had done OK because there was that reassuring "thwack-rattle" when I make solid contact. I looked at my pro for more reassurance but was met with a puzzled expression.

"Hit another one," he told me, holding his chin up Jack Benny-style.

I did. Two "thwack-rattles" in a row. Wow.

"Sounds funny," he said.

Sounds? What about straight and true? What about proper release? What about –?

He took my club. "The grip end of your shaft is broken."

My heart sank. I played with borrowed golf shoes until last year. I write for a living. My budget for golf equipment fits somewhere between the money I set aside for underwear and the money I set aside for new ties. I have a family to feed. Did I need a new driver?

"We can probably just cut it down a bit," he said as we headed toward the pro shop.

As I forced myself to consider the possibility of new gear, he gave the driver to one of his young assistants. Thousands of advertisements for new clubs floated before my eyes.

Let's sort of role play, I suggested to my pro. I'm the guy who thinks he needs, oh, a new driver. Give me your pitch.

I was ready for the true meaning of sweet spots, cambered soles, torsion resistance and gear effects. I was also getting rather worked up.

"First thing I do is determine the level of interest and ability," he began. "I don't try to debate the ads. I explain the variations of the equipment and what to expect from it."

Boring, boring, boring. What's the real difference?

Let's sort of role play, I suggested to my pro. I'm the guy who thinks he needs, oh, a new driver. Give me your pitch.

"Honestly?" he asked, the bemused look of the teacher replacing the salesman's guile.

Of course! I cried, my whole body trembling with anticipation.

"Price," he said.

What about investment cast heads, graphite, boron, beryllium? What about epoxy-faced plates, or personally imprinted golf tees? I asked. Foam was beginning to develop around the corners of my mouth.

"The average golfer doesn't usually break 100," he said.

"What do you really need to knock a few strokes off your game?"

Titanium shafts? I suggested. Better perimeter weighting?

"Lessons and practice," he replied simply.

What a sense of humor. Here I was, ready to get a lesson in metallurgy and aerodynamics, and I'm told that head mass and torque resistance aren't that important?

"People buy clubs for the same reasons they buy anything else," he continued. "Prestige, status, utility and price, in relation to the grocery bill. But to really get any better it takes lessons and practice," he concluded as the young assistant returned my driver.

"Gee, I haven't see one of these in a long time," the assistant said. "The top of the shaft was cracked and a piece had broken off. Made kind of a rattle when you swung it. Oh, and I re-whipped your hosel. It was coming loose."

I beg your pardon? I said. That's when I learned what you call the place where the long part of the club (shaft) fits into the part that hits the ball (head). The hosel.

My pro and I walked back out to the tee. I swung at a few. The nice "thwack" sans "rattle" was disconcerting at first. I hit several balls reasonably straight, just fore and aft of the 200-yard flag. I was astonished.

"You'll get the idea with a little practice," my pro smiled.

I hit several more. Get the idea? (Thwack!) With this old stick? (Thwack!) If I could get 200 straight yards with this ancient (Thwack!) clunker, just imagine what I could do with a precision-designed instrument! (Thwack!)

I knew I could do without a tie. I just wondered (Thwack!) if I could make my underwear last another year. ■

The Balls of Golf

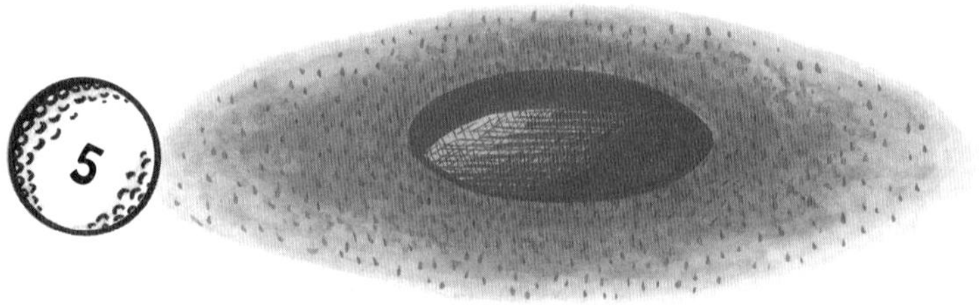

My pro has this really great habit of picking up lost balls on the golf course and giving them to me. He averages about 12 per month, which is my approximate rate of consumption. He gives them to me because he won't let me borrow his.

That's because my pro uses balata balls. No, this is not a Greek musical instrument. A balata ball (named after the rubbery stuff on the cover) is a $2 to $3 golf ball that is supposed to give the player better feel and control. (You've seen those impossible shots on television where the ball sort of backs into the hole.)

Balata balls are not found stacked 20 boxes high on the floor of the pro shop. They're usually the ones found on a shelf behind the cash register about two boxes deep. Golfers who use balata balls don't need many because they don't lose them. These players use words like "birdie" and phrases like "six under for the day." They also mark their balls with little identifying lines or dots so there's never any question about whose ball it is in the fairway (balata balls always seem to end up in the fairway). Which, of course, is why I was so desperate to try one.

So, what sort of ball do you think I should use? I asked my pro. We were in his office and preparing to play a few holes together.

"The ones I give you," he said as he handed me yet another assortment of the balls he had found. Along with their brand name, several of them advertised various automobiles, insurance companies and liquors.

But I mean, what if I were to actually, you know, buy a box of balls?

"Why would you want to do that?" he asked, mildly surprised. My pro knows me well enough. I seldom use the word "buy" in reference to anything having to do with the game of golf.

Well, I replied, dragging my toe back and forth across his carpet like a teenager asking for a date, I was reading this ad about a new balata with a dimple pattern that gives you a tour trajectory –

"You're reading *ads* again?" His voice was raised above his normal calm delivery.

– And superior in-flight performance, I concluded.

"I will let you use a balata when you can play the same ball for 36 holes straight," he said. "Shoot under 90 both games, with no mulligans." He smiled. "And pay the $32."

My foot stopped. My head dropped. My eyes closed. That was impossible.

"OK, I'll pay the $32," he said.

I couldn't decide if it was the foot, head or the eye-closing bit, but now I had an almost achievable goal: one ball and a couple of 89s. I could already see my balata backspinning into the cup.

My pro teed up, aiming the name on his balata ball (a new Titleist) down the target line. Two hundred fifty yards later it stopped in the middle of the fairway.

I teed up. I aimed the name of my ball (a Glenlivet).

It took us a few minutes, but we found my Glenlivet nestled in a pile of leaves off to the right. I was ecstatic. Only 177 more strokes stood between me and my first balata. ■

The Best Excuse

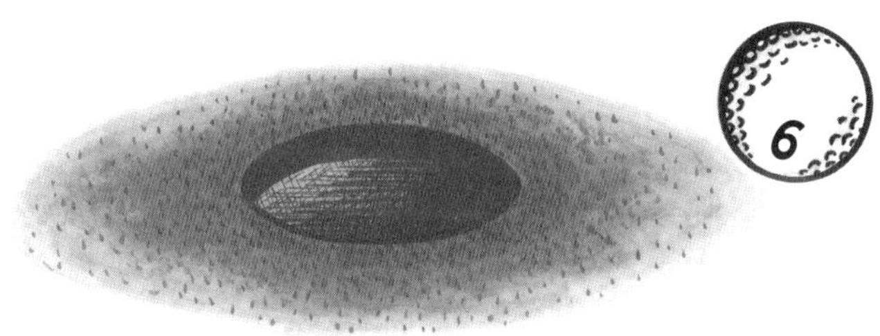

Golf may be the most democratic game in the great pantheon of sports, my pro told me when I wondered aloud why a 30-handicapper (i.e., a duffer) would pay a $200 greens fee to suffer through 18 hellish holes of a course like, say, Pebble Beach, when he or she could suffer just as much at a $15-a-round goat-ranch course instead, cart included.

"It's the second shot," my pro said. He can be annoyingly cryptic at times. I waited.

"The famous courses, the ones with the big fees, the ones you see on television where the touring pros play," he began.

Yes? I said.

"Well, after your drive, that second shot is exactly what Nicklaus or Watson or Kite faces in a tournament. You face what they face. You're equal to the best. That's the democracy of golf," he explained. "And you can buy it."

You sound like a real estate salesman selling swampland, I said, unable to accept his logic. I'll tell you what's democratic about golf.

There was what can only be described as a pregnant pause as my pro concentrated on his putt while biting his lip. He knew I was about to launch into what he considers my "passion for the trivialities of the game."

Excuses, I exclaimed, trying to sound as enigmatic as he had a moment ago. Since he was still biting his lip, I continued.

There is a treasure trove of excuses that we, as golfers, can use for every shot we mess up. These excuses work, whether we are raking in a few million a year playing the game or always filling in three digits on our score cards. And they are accepted by all other golfers.

For example, I continued, there's Ray Floyd on television after he dumps one in a creek from a horrible lie under a tree. "I caught a tree root," Floyd tells the viewers. Raymond, they all respond, I too have caught a tree root. I too have dumped one in the creek. I have empathy. I suffer with you. We are equal, Ray. May I call you Ray?

Hairy greens, tree roots, wind, sun, rain, shoes too tight – all these glorious excuses. We never have to confess responsibility or that we just plain blew it or that we're incompetent. We can say, along with Ray, we caught a tree root, and we're exonerated. Golf excuses are democracy in action, I finished.

My pro sank his 10-foot putt. I have always admired the way he could sink putts while chuckling.

I walked over to my ball, four feet from the cup, and studied my intended path. The first thing that crossed my mind was that, three times out of four, I miss four-foot putts. My second thought was, What believable excuse could I use if I missed? My pro was a bit of a stickler about such things.

Then it came to me. The hat trick of all excuses. The "grain of the green." The grain, I knew, was the direction in which the grass was lying. Kind of like the hair on your head. If you putt with the grain, your ball rolls faster. Putt against it and the ball slows down. In all my golfing life, although I've worried about my wife, children, car payments and income taxes, I have never worried about the grain. This seemed the perfect excuse.

I putted. My ball stopped 12 inches short.

My pro shook his head slowly. "Good alignment, good stroke. I guess you didn't notice you were putting against the grain."

Without question, the best excuse of all. Are you with me, Ray? ■

Overcoming Bag Drop

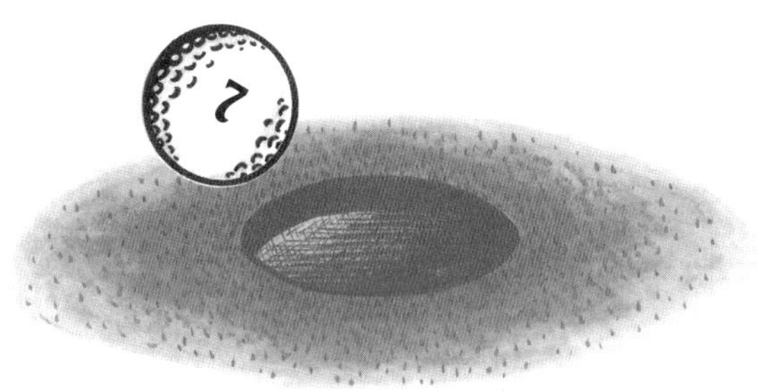

For the novice, intimidation might seem to be a requisite part of golf. As an example, every new golfer suffers from FTMD (First Tee Melt Down). The cause is simple enough.

The first tee is invariably placed within view of the pro shop, where all those waiting golfers hold vigil. Beginners know in their bones (which are shaking uncontrollably) that everyone is waiting for them to whiff the ball and dampen their drawers.

The remedy is also simple. Reverse the front nine. Put the first tee out in the boonies, away from those thousands of beady little eyes boring into you as you make your third attempt to drive the ball past the tee box. It takes the pressure off.

I brought this up to my pro while we were hitting balls off the practice tee in one of my rare appearances on this part of the course. Even rarer was the fact that the following day I was actually going to play for the first time in almost a month.

"Nobody cares what you do off the first tee unless you're slowing up starting times," my pro replied as he nailed one with his seven iron, the trajectory of the ball forming a perfect arc and just brushing the 150-yard flag.

I offered my argument after nailing one with my seven iron considerably more to the right (I thought it rather excessive the way the golfers scurried off the tee as my ball passed well in front of them).

FTMD (see above), I said, is actually the culmination of various degradations the novice must endure prior to approaching the first tee.

"Like what?" my pro asked as another one of his balls soared into perfect orbit, like NASA at its best. My ball, feeling obliged to go somewhere after being slapped so indecorously by my seven iron, spun viciously to the left. The folks at NASA would have pushed the self-destruct button.

OK, I began, let's start with the approach.

"How can that be intimidating?" he asked. "You just get behind the ball, line it up with the target –"

No, no, no, I interrupted. I mean the approach to the clubhouse. We're talking *real* fundamentals here.

That quieted him down. He's big on fundamentals.

Take the little signs the beginning golfer sees as he or she drives up.

"Signs?" he asked.

As a beginning golfer, I said, you have read everyone from Jones to Penick (i.e., Bob and Harvey). You have completely ignored wife, husband, lover and/or children while you devoured the first issue of your new subscription to *Golf Digest*. You have strapped onto your body so many appliances to improve your swing that the Marquis de Sade would jump for joy. But no one ever told you what to do when you reached the bag drop.

By the way my pro's eyes rolled back in his head, I knew I was getting somewhere.

As you advance up the drive, little signs with arrows guide you inescapably to a small area that may or may not include other bags. Your mind is flooded with cautionary advice gleaned from the books, articles and videos so recently consumed.

Do I lose or gain a stroke if I leave my bag at the bag drop?

As you advance up the drive, little signs with arrows guide you inescapably to a small area that may or may not include other bags.

What if I just carry my bag to the pro shop? Is there a penalty? Do I park first, or do I head straight for the bag drop first?

It was obvious my pro was visibly shaken by my revelations. At least he was shaking visibly.

"Where do you get this stuff?" he asked, his smile now a full-fledged laugh.

Personal experience, I responded, perhaps too quickly. Something must be done! I said. My upper lip had Nixonesque perspiration covering it.

"You sure get worked up when you haven't played in a while. How about if I just meet you out in the parking lot tomorrow?" he suggested.

I was reminded again of just how gentlemanly and insightful my pro can be. ■

You Can't Fool Mother

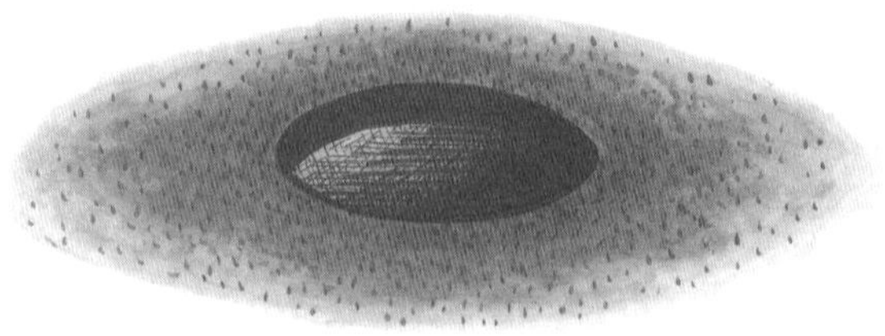

Seven years ago, when my wife was pregnant and I took up golf, her favorite activity was watching the Weather Channel. I thought she was the only human being on earth who could actually watch the Weather Channel for an entire day and enjoy it.

When we attended the hospital's child preparedness classes (notice how close the name is to "hurricane preparedness"), I discovered that many other pregnant women watched the Weather Channel religiously. My wife explained it had something to do with a pregnant woman's closeness to nature.

Right, I said sarcastically.

"Right," she replied with that knowing glow of a woman with child (in our case, children).

The problem is, she still watches the Weather Channel religiously.

"And what does this have to do with golf?" my pro asked last week when he came out to watch me tee off. Since there was no thunder or lightning, they were allowing us to play in the heavy drizzle. Like the guys in my foursome, my pro was dressed in a very neat rain suit, the kind that doesn't mess up

your swing. I own the old-fashioned kind of rain suit. It's called an umbrella, although I seemed to have forgotten it today.

"What does your wife and the Weather Channel –?"

When is the last time it rained on this course? I asked.

He thought for a moment. "When was the last time you played?"

He was getting the picture.

My wife loves to play golf. Since she's the one who gets to be with the kids most of the time, she may love to play golf more than I do. The world being as it is, she just doesn't get as many chances as I do. But she can control the weather.

Somebody asks me to play golf. I'm supposed to be cleaning out the garage or going to an important business meeting or making the mortgage payment. I know I can sneak off for four hours and the world will not end. Do I tell my wife where I'm going? Do you?

So I sneak off. And it rains. Or the temperature drops 30 degrees. If I'm on a really fancy private course (one my wife would abandon the children to get a chance to play), the barometric pressure plunges to what the people on the Weather Channel call a "tropical depression," and gale-force winds accompany my wife's precipitation.

I know this weather business is my wife's doing because it's unexpectedness makes the paper the next day. The headline usually reads, "Freak Storm Washes Out Two Holes At (name of course I played)."

When I finished my story, my pro shook his head. "Why don't you just tell your wife you're playing golf?"

I reflected a moment.

As I walked toward the phone in the starter's booth, I noticed the clouds were beginning to break up. The rainbow over the first fairway was beautiful. ■

Condom Golf

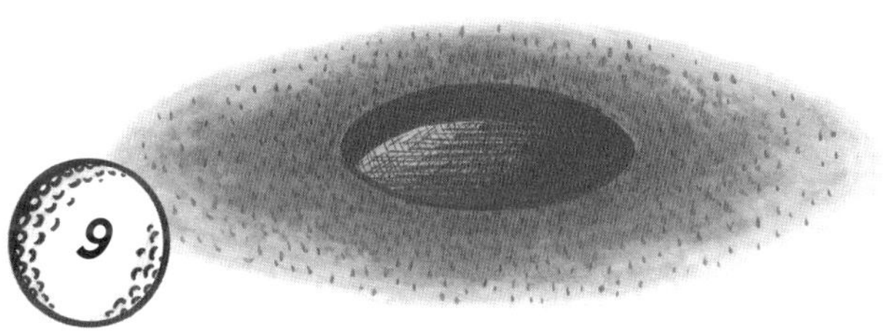

Until I learned about condom golf, I was easily seduced by a variety of temptations. Standing in a dense forest or facing a 200-yard carry over water, I would hear this sultry, Bo Derek-like voice say, "Show me what you've got, fella."

Until condom golf, killing trees and feeding fish were a regular part of my game.

On one occasion, a few days ago, I found myself in the trees. I could see the green about 80 yards ahead. Except for the low oak branch above me, a very tall pine to my right, some stumpy bushes in front and the gnarled root my ball lay behind, I had a pretty clear shot.

"You found it?" my pro asked as he stumbled through the underbrush. "I really thought that one was a goner."

We studied my situation. I looked at the voluptuous green again. Bo's top was about to drop. I had to act.

I yanked my three iron out of my bag.

"Guess you're going to try to make it?" he asked quietly, moving toward one of the pines.

I knew I was taking a chance but, heck, it was only a game. I'd seen Nicklaus and Ballesteros do it. I'd seen my older brother try it. The odds, two out of three, were in my favor.

I looked around for my pro. I checked the big pine to the right. He was there, his body one with the bark.

"The *safe* shot," he said slowly, "would be to chip it back down the fairway."

Back? As in reverse? As in toward the tee?

Seven strokes and three trees later, we were on our way to the next hole, a spectacular, extraordinary and admittedly tempting dog-leg right, par five.

The spectacular part was the beautiful lake bordering the left.

Two of my shots landed in the fairway. Extraordinary.

Now the tempting part. There was the beguiling green, hemmed in on the left by a finger of that marvelous lake and by a large sand bunker in front. Coming off the lake was what I judged to be about a 20-knot wind. Very invigorating. I could see the wind in Bo's hair.

The pin, of course, was far left, the maw of the trap facing me. I was seduced.

I lined up with the pin. The wind howled. I could taste par. I could feel its caress, could hear its song. Song? No, it was more like a shout. It was tough to tell in that gale. I listened again. It was definitely a shout. My pro, already on the green, was shouting.

"RRRIIIIIGHT!" he yelled.

What? I shouted back.

He rushed over to me. "Right," he repeated, somewhat out of breath.

Right what?

"What is the safe shot?" he asked.

I looked at the voluptuous green again. Bo's top was about to drop. ... I yanked my three iron out of my bag.

Looking to my right I noticed 18 acres of green. Right? I asked.

"A ha!"

But the pin? But par?

I safely pitched a 30-foot shot to the green. It landed as far from the pin as possible.

I safely putted the ball. It stopped four feet short of the hole. I counted my strokes. One. Two. Three. Four.

Four?

The King of Three-Putt counted again, very slowly.

Four strokes. Four feet. In the hole.

A ha.

I played condom golf the rest of the day. ■

Cry Wolf

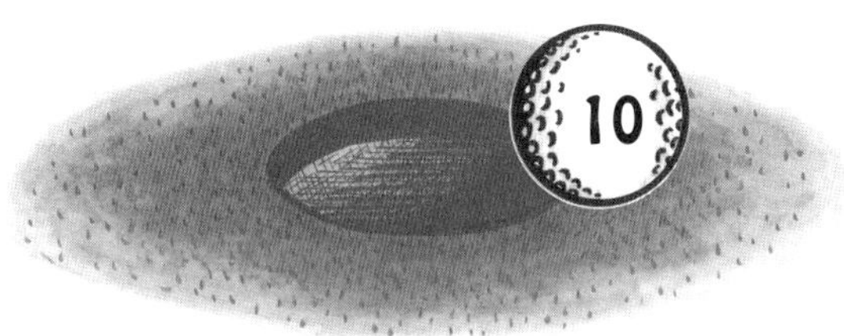

When I was a kid, I used to bet on the Chicago Cubs. The team has yet to recover. It's not that I'm unlucky, but when it comes to me wagering money, check the Cub's statistics for the past 40 years.

Which is why I seldom bet in golf. Which is why the other day, when one of our foursome said, "Let's play 'Wolf,'" I was nonplused. Quite purposefully, I know virtually nothing about the various ways of placing bets in golf. Except for Nassaus.

"No more!" my pro had said rather forcefully a few weeks back after working out a settlement of 10 cents on the dollar for my past due in Nassaus.

Absolutely! I'd promised, relieved he did not make me go to a Gamblers Anonymous meeting. Again.

"You have enough of a problem keeping track of your score," he'd said, "let alone whether you're up or down two. And you're too easy to con."

Quite right, I'd agreed. How could I have argued with him? After all, he was paying off my debt with his money.

Which is why I felt rather uncomfortable when my playing partner said, "Wolf is really simple. And a lot of fun."

The last time I had "fun"

like that, my children's college fund had been in jeopardy. But my partner would not be dissuaded. "We'll play for just a quarter a point," he persisted.

From experience, I presently deposited $2 in the bottom of my golf bag (enough for the milk I was to bring home after the game) where it would be difficult for me to get at. I then tried to listen as my partner told me how points in Wolf were accumulated. My eyes began to glaze over as he explained the rules, but I came to attention when he said, "And if you want to play against the other three, you say, 'Wolf, Wolf, Wolf,' at the tee."

I was having a difficult time controlling myself. Four grown men running around a golf course yelling Wolf, Wolf, Wolf?

What? I laughed.

"Wolf, Wolf, Wolf," he repeated.

I was having a difficult time controlling myself. Four grown men running around a golf course yelling Wolf, Wolf, Wolf?

"You don't have to yell it," my partner said. He was serious. I couldn't resist.

I always consider the front nine a kind of practice round, at least that's what I tell my wife when I get a chance at an additional nine. The first three holes of my practice round were typical in that I had already lost one ball. Yet, due to the rather esoteric rules of Wolf golf, I had somehow accumulated points (i.e., quarters). I was amazed.

"You just got three because Ben here blew his putt," my partner explained.

It was the next hole, a par three, that did it. One of the guys actually said, "Wolf, Wolf, Wolf," out loud. Really loud. I bit my lip. My eyes started to water. Doing my best to hold back a laugh, I swung freely at my ball. It landed on the green. Two more strokes (though it should have been one), and I got par and three more points.

I never had the courage to say Wolf, Wolf, Wolf myself. But when I stopped at the grocery store on the way home, I had enough money to buy milk, bread and a very small bottle of very inexpensive wine. ■

Bag of Evidence

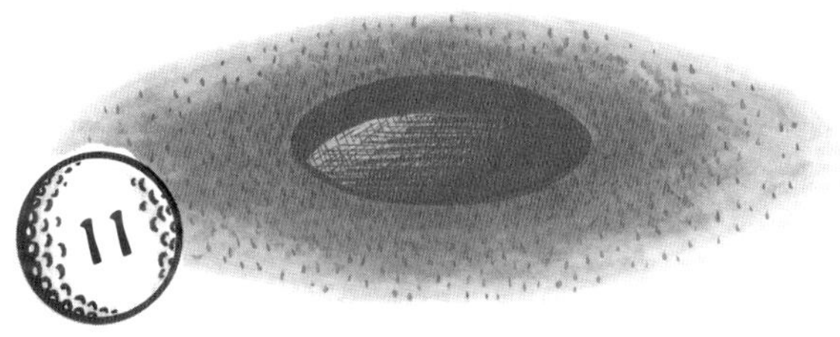

When my pro suggested I try my skills in a tournament he was holding at the club, I told him I would rather take the high road and not dirty myself on the underside of golf. I had heard rumors about gentlemen, even ladies, who pumped their handicaps up into the 20s and 30s then shot a career game in the low 80s, a golf tradition known as sandbagging. Dirty stuff.

Plus, I said, I estimated I already owed a number of his members over $200 dollars in unpaid 25-cent Wolf points. Despite my initial success in the game, my luck had apparently run out.

"Two hundred dollars?" my pro exclaimed. "That means you would have had to have lost virtually every hole in every game you've played in the past two years!"

I know, I said. I'm starting to get threatening phone calls.

He laughed, knowing my sense of humor. I admitted I might be a little off on my estimate. I did not admit it was probably on the low side.

"A tournament can really help your game," he said seriously.

How? I asked.

"Well, if you're the competitive sort ..."

I drifted off. Competitive? I compete with my wife for the bathroom each morning. After

more than a decade of connubial bliss, I'm one down in this never-ending tournament we've been having.

Competitive? When we only had one television (that worked) I pretended "Cartoon Express" was an animated version of McNeil-Lehrer. The kids or my beloved always got the clicker.

"... So you see," my pro concluded, "it just might do you some good. Anyway, I'm one short of a full field."

The entry fee was $30. After a few subtle words of encouragement, my pro agreed to front me the money.

Any tips? I asked, steeling myself against the mortification I knew would soon follow. To think my score would be posted in public view sent me into a semi-catatonic state.

"Make sure your foursome includes the guy with the new tour bag, club tubes and clean towel," my pro said smiling.

A tour bag, I remembered, is the big one that has a little over 800 pockets, straps and belts. It also weights about 800 pounds. The tubes are long plastic things designed to keep clubs protected and separated in the bag. (Note to fishermen: With the ends sliced off at the appropriate angle, the tubes – found in most water hazards on the back nine – are of tremendous value. Stab the pointy end into a river bank or beach; the exposed end holds a fishing rod quite nicely.)

"Stick to him like glue if he has head covers that look like little fluffy animals," my pro continued.

The kind you sell in your pro shop? I asked.

He did not smile. "If he has the latest oversized driver in his bag, plus a three, five and seven wood, uses balata balls and immediately starts talking about the grain of the green," he concluded, "you may have a chance."

A chance at what? I asked. At winning? Was this guy a Golfing Great? – a person who, by my simple association with him, would make me a Nick Faldo or Jack Nicklaus or Barry Bonds?

My pro reminded me that Bonds played baseball. I knew that. I was just excited.

"Not quite," my pro said, almost sadly. "I have just described the ultimate duffer. The guy who can't hit his way out of a paper bag. The guy whose grown-up kids give him every golf gadget in the world for Christmas because he's a golfer and they've forgotten who he really is. The guy who, no matter what handicap he admits, will shoot higher. Much higher. He always does."

And I'm supposed to learn from this? I asked.

"No," my pro replied flatly. "He's your guarantee you won't have the highest score."

Out of the corner of my eye I saw a fluffy little puppy dog head covering an oversized driver, the biggest I'd ever seen. I turned back to my pro.

He nodded.

I went over to meet my new partner. ■

Surfing the Fairways

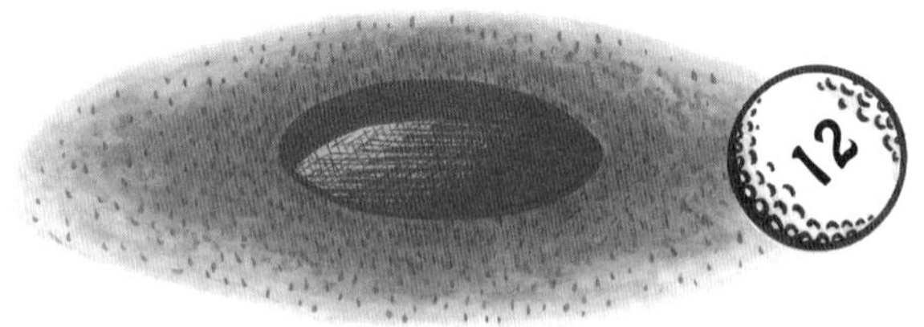

There is now a high-tech gizmo you can carry around in your pocket that will tell you the precise distance between you and the pin (i.e., the stick with the flag on it) from anywhere on the fairway. "The finest aid to club selection," the brochure says.

> *As I begin to add up my score card (I carry a small calculator in my bag), I marvel at science.*

I click the little gizmo. From the front of the oak, it says I am 137.2 yards from the pin. From behind the oak where my ball is it's 138.2 yards from the pin.

I am tempted to use my low-tech foot wedge to get my ball into better position. However, being a golfer of honor (the fact that my opponent is three feet away and watching my every move has nothing to do with my decision), I use a nine iron to pop it back into the fairway (145.6 yards from the pin).

I flawlessly execute a seven iron to the green. It is a broad green. I am still 11.3 yards from the hole.

I pull out another gizmo from my bag: my putter. According to the advertisement, and for $169.95, it will effortlessly assist my ball into the hole from this distance. My ball is assisted three times before it disappears beneath the green.

As I begin to add up my score card (I carry a small calculator in my bag), I marvel at science. I also return the little distance gizmo and the $169.95 putter I'd borrowed from my pro.

"Well, what do you think?" he asks.

I think I may need to fine tune my game a little, I reply dispassionately.

"You mean you actually want a lesson?"

My pro has a sense of humor. Like practicing, taking a formal lesson strikes me as admitting defeat. No, I tell him, I'm going to surf the Net.

"What?" he asks.

Of the 50 million or so computer hackers who are wired up to the "World Wide Web," one of them must have a technological remedy for my putting, I explain.

The Web, or Internet, is, of course, mankind's great leap onto the information superhighway. Millions of computers (and their operators) are linked together via phone lines and modems, discussing the existence of God or whether Debi@ios.com (user's Web address) would consider a blind date with Bart@aol.com.

An admitted techno-junkie, I rush home to my computer and post a question on the GOLFHELP.winusa.com bulletin board (I visualize these electronic bulletin boards as big refrigerator doors floating around in the ether with all kinds of little yellow Post-it Notes on them). I put my question before 50 million computer jockeys: What do I do about my putting?

The following day, I review my electronic mail box, expecting it to be filled with magnificent, high-tech breakthroughs that will solve my three-putt problems.

I have received two messages. The first, BART@aol.com wants a date. The second reads simply, "Meet you on the front practice green at 2:15 p.m. YOURPRO@course.com." ■

Canadian Scoring

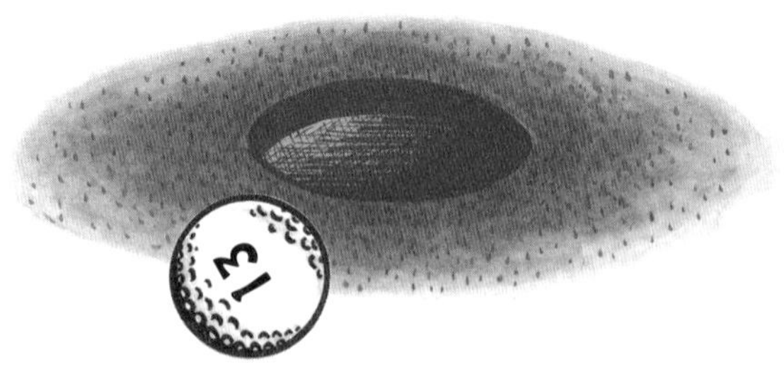

What we Americans know about Canada and Canadians could fill one entire side of a score card, if we wrote really big. We don't know that nation's capitol. If we pay attention at all, we're puzzled by that country's politics and postal system. Baseball? Blue Jays? World Series? U.S. baseball fans have already forgotten.

Inadvertently, my pro, who has actually played golf in Canada, led me to a great score-lowering concept based on our national ignorance of things Canadian.

It was a cold, blustery day in January on the little South Carolina island where I live. I was hanging out at the pro shop fingering new clubs I could never afford in hopes I might somehow talk my way into another free round of golf from one of the new assistant pros. (Note: Hit up new assistants for free games within two weeks of their first day on the job. They become jaded about giving away tee times after 14 days. That's also about the time the head pro identifies for the new assistant all the freeloaders who hang around the pro shop fingering – but never buying – new clubs.)

A foursome from Canada

came in to pay their cart and greens fees. I immediately knew their country of origin because they were wearing Bermudas and short-sleeved shirts. Everyone else in the shop was wearing parkas, it being a chilly 64 degrees.

My pro welcomed them.

"Take Canadian?" they asked.

My ears perked up. Would the club take Canadians? As far as I knew, this was an equal-opportunity 18 holes. I'd never heard anyone say Canadians were barred from play. It took me a second to realize they were talking about money.

Would the club take Canadians? As far as I knew, this was an equal-opportunity 18 holes. I'd never heard anyone say Canadians were barred from play.

My pro, ever the diplomat, agreed to a reasonable exchange rate, 76 cents per Canadian dollar. The foursome, giving my pro a friendly hard time about the expense of golf in The States, offered him a wad of funny-colored money and hurried out, fingering nothing.

At first, the episode didn't affect me. But when I started fingering my fourth driver, I started translating its outrageous price into what would be the even more outrageous Canadian price. I was nearly struck dumb! (My wife would say "dumber.") In that instant, I developed Canadian Scoring.

The concept is simple, but you have to be quick. At the end of your game, announce you are going to use the Canadian scoring system for your final score. Tell your partners it is fairly based on the fiduciary relationship between the U.S. and Canada. Your partners, impressed that you know how to say fiduciary, let alone that you might know what it means, will agree.

Then explain quickly, as you pencil in your total, that the 100 on your scorecard represents the value of a Canadian dollar in Canada. However, since you're playing in the U.S., it's actually worth only 76.

From experience, I suggest using the method sparingly. ■

In the Garden of Good and Evil and Someone Else's

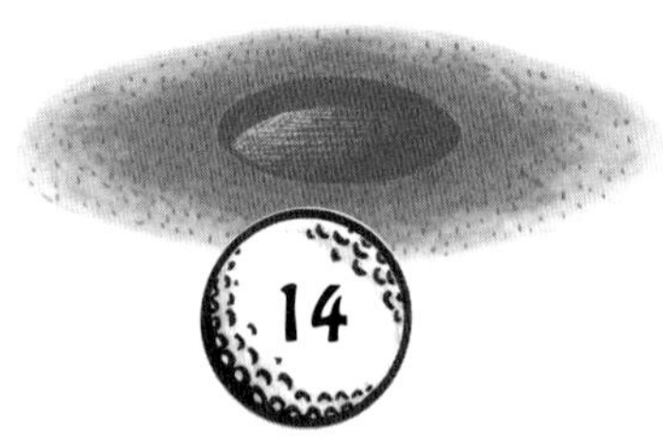

There is a best-selling murder mystery with a name similar to the above. Based on an informal survey I recently took, odds are that you, as a golfer, haven't read it. Out of five foursomes interviewed (i.e., 20 people), no one had read *Midnight In The Garden of Good and Evil* by John Berendt. After all, the murder weapon was not a golf club.

As a golfer, who has time to read? You spend a minimum of five hours every week frustrating yourself on the golf course. You spend five hours per week taking that frustration out on your family, significant other, etc. You spend five more hours apologizing to the above, and another five hours thinking up plausible excuses as to why you must play in this Friday's tournament rather than go to work, to a wedding, funeral, traffic court, dentist or shopping. Who has the time?

I had the time. I was playing in a tournament. The morning of the event, my wife told me we were going to get rained out. (My wife knows these things. Score for the past month: My Wife 7, Weather Channel 4.) She stashed the book, along with my umbrella, in my bag.

The sky was a crystal, cloudless blue.

The cold front moved in at the approximate speed of my ball as it sailed down the fairway on No. 1. Since there was no lightning, my cart partner and I decided to wait it out. Normally, this would have been a pleasant time for me (I enjoy good conversation as much as good golf). However, my cart partner was, I learned as he nodded off to sleep, an emergency-room physician who had spent the last 30 hours saving lives.

As the rain beat down, I pulled the book out of my bag. Four chapters later, the tournament director rolled up in his cart and told us to get moving.

I moved my ball from the center of the fairway into a garden, using what I call my "power fade." (My pro calls it my "gruesome slice.") It was a good and evil flower garden. The good part was that no trees blocked my shot. The evil part was that the gardener was actually in the garden, working on early fall flowers in the early fall drizzle. He looked very familiar, like an older version of my ... couldn't be.

"How in the (expletive deleted) did you manage to get from the middle of the fairway in here?" he demanded. "Your ball trashed my (expletive deleted) *Lycoris squamigera!*"

From the look in his eyes, there was no mystery (see book above). There was, gauging from the menacing way he was holding his clippers, a very serious possibility of murder. I found some comfort in my cart partner's profession.

Power fade, I replied, hoping my eloquent golf terminology would impress this fellow in dirty overalls.

"That was the most gruesome slice I've ever seen! You're not releasing through the ball. And from what I could see, you were aligned to the right, anyway," the gardener huffed. "Give me that thing!"

He demonstrated proper release a few times then returned my club, grip first. I apologized, thanked him, took my drop, aligned, swung and released through the ball. It landed close to the green, more or less where I was aiming.

I turned to wave my thanks to the gardener. A younger man was standing next to him. He was wearing my pro's shoes, slacks, shirt, rain jacket, visor and face. They both waved back. ■

Easy Shots

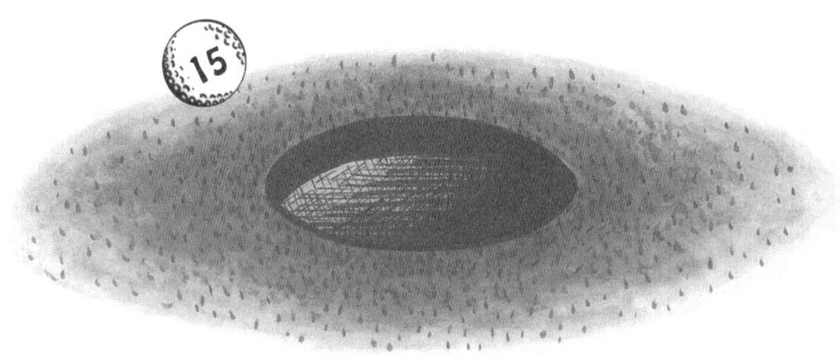

I was tired of hearing golf pros and players with single-digit handicaps tell me a sand shot (i.e., the shot you attempt when your ball decides to take up residence in a sand bunker) is, and I quote, "the easiest shot in golf." I happen to know there is no easy shot in golf. There are good shots and bad shots, difficult shots, impossible shots and preposterous shots. But easy shots? Not even close.

This topic came up as my pro and I watched, from a distance, a popular pediatrician viciously throw his ball into a nearby water hazard after several attempts to float it out of a greenside bunker.

"That's such an easy shot," my pro lamented. He wasn't being snotty. He was feeling genuinely sorry for the doctor.

I suggested that being in sand traps changed a person. The sand made golfers do strange things. For instance, I said, I doubt our pediatrician would, after several unsuccessful attempts to quiet a colicky baby, hurl the infant into a lake. The sand makes us act differently than we normally do. And after you mess up the sand trying to slap your ball out of there, you are required, by the honorable codes of golf, to fluff up the sand with a special tool so the next miserable sod who finds his ball in there suffers the same fate you did. Funny game.

"Even some good golfers seem to go brain dead the moment their feet touch the sand," my pro agreed. "But I think it's mostly because they don't understand the concept."

The concept, I said, is to get you *irritated*.

"Not the concept of the bunker," he retorted. "I mean the concept of the sand shot."

The concept, I re-retorted, is still to get you *irritated*. I have seen priests break sand wedges across their holy knees after a series of unsuccessful attempts to lift one out of the little granules. I have heard sainted grandmothers, after being foiled by sand, use language that would embarrass the most rabid rap musician. I have heard from very reliable golf course superintendents that cats won't even use a sand trap for a litter box because of the evil vibrations the bunker gives off.

The doctor and his partner had cleared the green (and most of the sand from one of the bunkers). My pro pitched his shot straight at the pin, which was positioned on the front of the green and very near another greenside bunker. A slight breeze stirred just as his ball reached the top of its graceful arc, killing the ball's forward motion. An otherwise perfect shot plopped into the fluffy white sand.

About 10 yards back from where my pro's ball had been, I ripped a seven iron at the flag. My ball landed just a few yards short and four feet to the right of my pro's ball, in the sand. I went brain dead.

"Just watch," he told me.

I watched. He took a mighty swing, and the ball floated out of the bunker and onto the green. It disappeared into the hole. What was even more remarkable was that he had not even hit the ball. He'd hit the sand. I had seen it. He had failed to hit the ball.

"That's the concept," my pro explained. "The sand actually lifts the ball. Your clubface never touches it."

Hit the sand? I asked, awaiting reassurance.

"Yep," he said. "Be brave."

This is what I love about golf. I now get to hit the sand – *hard*. All these years of pent-up anger, all those shots hopelessly thwarted, and now I get to beat this vile sand into submission.

Finally, I am at peace. ■

Locals Rule

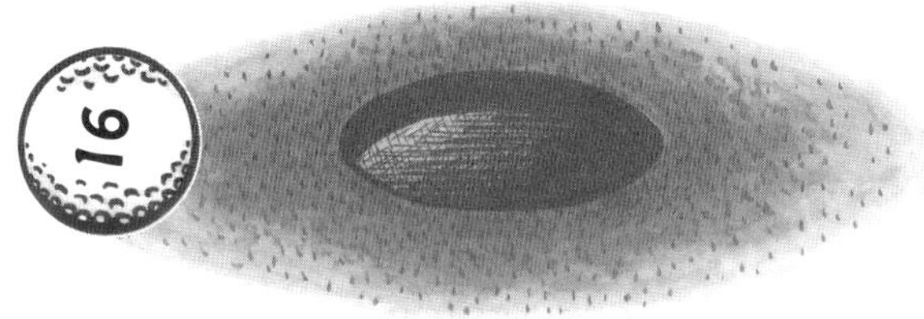

I have discovered a sure-fire way to advance through 18 holes and improve your score – without bringing down upon thy head "(expletives deleted)" from the foursome hot on your tail. I call it "locals rule."

As often happens, I must credit my pro with the genesis of the idea. I must also credit my continued interest in the rough to my right, for one day this rough included an alligator. Alligators are a common sight on my home course. What was uncommon was the relationship between my ball and the reptile: namely, about six inches. From snout to tail, the gator, one of his eyes glaring at me, measured at least eight feet.

Sensing my discomfort, my pro suggested the local rule. As indicated on my scorecard, it stated I was entitled to a free drop (i.e., no additional strokes would be added to my score) a safe distance from that potentially lethal snout, but no closer to the hole. I suggested the fairway on No. 17. We were on No. 5.

My safely distanced free drop actually put me in scoring position. A lucky shot put me on the green. Out of the corner of my eye, I saw the gator move. Fear put my ball in the hole.

"Ought to have more gators in your game," my pro mused as he marked down my par as we approached the next hole.

Ought to have more local rules, I replied ... which got me thinking.

Who creates these local rules? I asked my pro as we did a rather neat grid search for my ball in the trees to the right.

"Common sense," he answered.

I thought of other opportunities to use local rules (i.e., common sense) on the course. But you would have to be careful who you played with (i.e., no locals).

I tried it out the next day. Fortunately, I was paired up with a guy from Minnesota. He hit it a country mile off the first tee. I didn't. From the sound of the breaking glass, common sense dictated I stay away from that side of the fairway.

I took a drop to the far left. My partner, being friendly, just smiled.

Local rule, I explained. Houses built too close to the

fairway are considered ground under repair.

On the next hole I hit a classic. Sprinkler head to cart path to tree trunk and right into some muck that was sure to be infested with poisonous snakes.

As I took another free drop I explained the local rule about the Wetlands Protection Act.

My partner shrugged again, sans smile.

By No. 4, my partner seemed to be growing envious of my local knowledge, since I had taken advantage of my common-sense approach on three more occasions. I could tell by the way he wasn't speaking to me.

Now the real beauty of "locals rule" is that, as a local, you can share your common sense. My partner gruffly yanked his driver out of the bag and walked up to the No. 5 tee. As luck would have it, his shot cannoned off to the right in the direction of my alligator from the previous day.

My partner was much more accurate than I had been. His ball hit the creature between those bulbous eyes.

As we ran to the next tee, my partner gasped, "Didn't know they could run that fast!"

Local rule says we both take birdies on that hole and this one, I explained as we continued to jog past the greens on Nos. 5 and 6.

"Ought to have more gators in your game," my pro mused as he marked down my par. …

After we caught our breath on No. 7, my partner asked me if there were any more local rules he should be made aware of. I told him that from now on we could both call them as we saw them.

My magnanimity was rewarded. His Minnesotan smile returned. ■

First Blood

My pro called me. That may seem inconsequential, but in the decade-plus I've known him, he has called me only twice before. Both calls had been in reference to his inability to give me a free lesson because someone was willing to pay him for a lesson at the time. Not only do I beg free greens fees but time on the lesson tee as well. Golf writers have pride of authorship, nothing more.

But this call was different. My six-year-old daughter took the message. I was deeply involved in a computer game with my six-year-old son (I was losing), and my daughter knew better than to interrupt our little contest.

"He wants to know if you're alright," my daughter said when the computer informed me I had been beaten yet again by the sweet-looking, blonde-haired, blue-eyed vicious little kid next to me.

What else did he say? I asked. Actually, I sort of yelled, which made my daughter cry, which made my son punch me on the arm (twins do that sort of thing) and tell me to "chill out." Several precious moments elapsed (I had to become an adult again, calm the waters, etc.) before I could ask what else my pro had said.

"He just wanted (sniff, sniff) to know (sniff, sniff) if you were (sniff, sniff) alright," my darling, distraught daughter finally got out.

"You can't play with the computer any more," my son told me, still punching me, as I dialed my pro.

You called? I asked, calm slowly returning to my voice.

"I haven't seen you in a while. I was a little concerned," my pro said.

I couldn't decide if he missed my free games, free lessons or my scintillating repartee. Then it hit me. It had been nearly two months since I had last played. I'll be right there, I told him and hung up.

I kissed the children (sniff, sniff, hit, hit), kissed my wife ("Where do you think you're –?"), kissed the dog (a mistake) and was at the clubhouse in just under five minutes.

"I didn't expect you so quickly," my pro said as I hefted my bag up to the practice tee, club in hand. Under normal driving conditions, the trip from my house to the course took 10 minutes.

I told him his call had triggered something, some primal response I couldn't control.

"First blood," he replied.

Beg pardon?

"This is your season opener, your Masters, your first game. You've been gorging yourself on all those tips and videos, dreaming all those dreams of par, those 250-yard drives. You want to get out there and –"

That would be *275* yards, I corrected. But he was right.

But then something happens. An alarm goes off. You start breathing rapidly. Your pulse shoots though the roof. You MUST play.

While I happened to live in a place where golf is played throughout the year, the number of games I usually play in what is referred to as "winter" here has decreased dramatically. Kids, school, business ... it all seems to pile up and games trail off.

But then something happens. An alarm goes off. You start breathing rapidly. Your pulse shoots though the roof. You MUST play.

You're right, I told my pro. I

must draw the first blood of the season – *now*.

I paused for a moment as I watched my first drive dribble off to the right, significantly shy of 275 yards. Luigi, I mumbled.

My pro looked puzzled. I explained as best I could.

Luigi is one of the two Mario brothers in a popular Nintendo game. My son always gets the character Mario, leaving me with Luigi. Luigi (me) never wins. But in golf, I have a chance.

"Yes," my pro replied as I knocked one straight and long, as much to my surprise as his. "In golf, you always have a chance." ■

At Home in Aruba

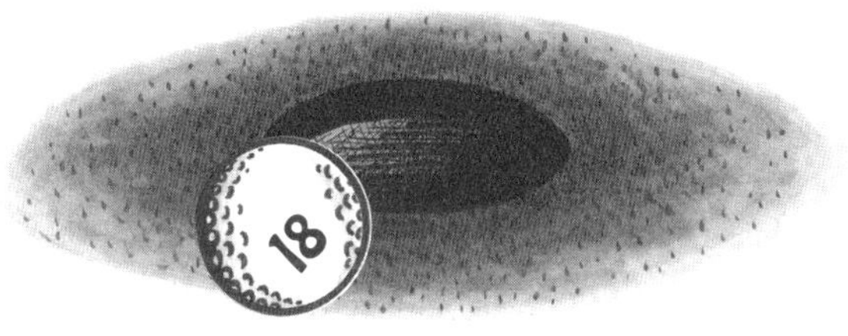

Golf writing has its good points and its bad points. One week you're up to your long irons in deadlines and the checks are rolling in. The next week you wonder if your phone number has been purposefully removed from every editor's Rollidex in the world. Which is what I was griping to my pro about when one of his assistants zoomed up in a cart and told me I had an important message at the clubhouse.

I became concerned. Family? IRS audit? Ed McMahon?

Forty-eight hours later, the captain informed us we would be arriving in Aruba 15 minutes early. On the port side of the plane, there was a gigantic rainbow. This has got to be some Steven Speilberg-inspired tourist gimmick, I thought, reminding myself that I couldn't let these cheap tricks influence my story.

The message hadn't been from my family, the IRS or Ed. The call had been from a very nice lady who had asked me if I wanted to write about a new golf course in Aruba.

I'd paused a moment. Aruba. Dutch Caribbean. Eighty-four degrees during the day. Every day. Seventy-four degrees at night. Every night. All desert. NEVER, NEVER rains.

People friendly to a fault.

This golf-writing assignment, I determined, had many good points. According to my itinerary, I would be whisked off to the beachfront Hyatt Regency (the white limo was a nice touch) where I would sit around drinking and eating while listening to our hosts' pitch about how beautiful the new course, Tierra del Sol, was.

By the end of the evening, I was able to enlighten the crowd on some of the finer details of the game. I found myself thankful that my pro wasn't around to do his embarrassing wincing when I started talking about golf.

Now the bad points. As my pro and I were looking for my second mulligan in the rough after initially learning of the trip, he said, "You know you'll have to play golf down there."

I'm used to his snide remarks. But the truth was, on a golf press trip, you do have to play golf. With scratch golfers. From the blue tees. Get real!

So there we were, our 8 a.m. tee time right on schedule. The course was immaculate, a bright green swath cut through the desert. In the distance, the deep blue Caribbean pounded against the shoreline.

I stood there, the last one up in our foursome. Three balls were already somewhere out there in the fairway. I pretended my pro was beside me, adjusting my alignment, stance, grip ...

Because it's a desert course, it's very easy to find your ball in the rough, amid the cacti, rocks and lizards. My bright white ball was nestled behind a small rock. Fortunately, the lizard was only stunned and scurried away when it saw me coming.

As I re-entered the fairway on my second shot, I decided to introduce my "floating mulligan" concept to Ray, my cart partner and the director of operations.

It's kind of mystical, I said, rather mystically. Ray gave me that quizzical look my pro always gives me when I come up with these concepts. I felt reassured.

"Floating?" Ray asked.

You see, when I play, no matter which tee I'm standing on, I always see this mulligan floating around near me, I said. And I just grab it when the need arises. There have been days when the need arose on all 18 holes. It speeds up play, I finished.

Ray shook his head (just like my pro) and smiled.

It didn't start raining until No. 5. I felt right at home. ■

Tempers Fugit

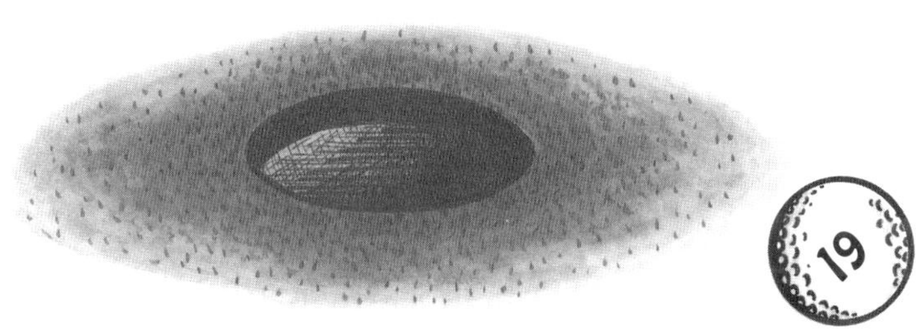

I am not, under normal circumstances, a violent person. Even in abnormal situations, I usually keep my cool. Like the time my then-four-year-old daughter spewed forth, a la *The Exorcist*, a three-hour car ride's worth of partially digested junk food and cherry cola all over the car and driver (me) the very moment we pulled into the drive of our beachside vacation house as dozens of cousins flung upon the doors, leaping for joy at our arrival. No sweat.

Now on the golf course ...

My pro and I watched a well-known and successful obstetrician sling his club into a nearby water hazard after a half-dozen failed attempts to escape a particularly deep bunker.

Wouldn't want him birthin' none of my babies, I said aloud.

"How do you do it?" he asked. ... "Three-putt here, four-putt there? I'd go crazy."

"True," my pro agreed, rather pensively. "Golf only magnifies what and who we already are. It may be the only sport we play that requires total honesty with ourselves. You

can't fake a good game."

Actually, I thought I was faking one pretty well. I was about to string three pars together. Due to a well-placed tree in the right-side rough, my somewhat misguided drive caromed off a branch and landed in the fairway. An easy nine iron to the pin.

"Tough luck," my pro said as I lifted my ball out of the cup six strokes later. I remained calm.

"How do you do it?" he asked. I calmly resisted the temptation to run him down with the golf cart. "Three-putt here, four-putt there? I'd go crazy."

To further resist an impulse to trample him with my spikes, I related an incident that had occurred a few years back.

My other pro – my wife – and I were playing with my older brother and his wife. Golf is one of the only recreational activities my brother and I can share. We live about two thousand miles apart. Golf draws us together.

My brother, I noticed, had developed something of a temper. Good-natured and charming off the course, he took a George Patton-like approach to his golf game. Pity those within earshot (or any shot) when he miscued. Being a natural mimic, I also started to loudly question the legal parentage of my ball, club and the course architect with every fluffed shot.

After four holes of my raving, my beloved got fed up.

"Why are you getting mad?" she asked.

#@%***!!, I shouted.

"Darling," she smiled, "you're not good enough to get mad."

#%&***!?, I asked.

"Now go over there, take your four cleansing breaths and strike the ball soundly," she said in her sultry Southern voice.

I took my four cleansing breaths (one of her Zen exercises) and soundly struck the ball out of the bunker.

Not good enough to get mad? I started to chuckle.

When I finished my tale, my pro ripped a tee shot almost out of sight. A rather violent gust of wind caught his ball mid-flight, steering it into a treacherous fairway bunker, a sight I'd seldom seen.

With a contorted, red face, he turned to me. "Four cleansing breaths?" he asked.

Works every time, I said. ■

Santa & Underwear

For Christmas, a friend of mine got a coffee cup that looks like a golf bag. If you're right-handed, it's safe. The coffee must only pass over the short irons and putter. For left-handers, it's more like a dribble glass. The driver and fairway woods extend well beyond the cup's lip.

Several years ago, my sister gave me a golf voodoo doll. … The three-putt area of my doll is in shreds.

Several years ago, my sister gave me a golf voodoo doll. There are little circles on it that say things like "three putt" and "worm burners." The three-putt area of my doll is in shreds.

Last Christmas, a friend of mine's ex-significant other gave her a two-hour-long video of outtakes from Tim Conway's Dorf on Golf series, "Not available (obviously) in stores." She's a three handicap.

Yet another friend received a battery-operated combination scorecard and tips booklet. The tips are based on signs of the Zodiac (typical tip: "Gemini: Select a putter or three wood.

Either will work in this situation").

There is (again, obviously) a plethora of gifts to give your golfer for Christmas. Though the electronic scorecard is truly a temptation (mention my name and get a 15 percent discount), I have a few meaningful suggestions based on years of observing the people who play the game.

First on my list is underwear. This goes for both ladies and gentlemen golfers. Plain old Jockey brand (mention my name, 10 percent discount) is fine. Rationale: When given a choice between new underwear and golf balls, golfers inevitably pick the latter.

Next, a subscription to any non-golf magazine. The focus of the publication should be personal relationships, sex or children. Rationale: Golfers do not participate in any of those activities. This may help broaden their horizons.

Finally, a photo album that includes pictures of those who are closest to the golfer (wife, husband, children, dog, cat, car, etc.). It should be small enough to fit into the pocket of a golf bag. Include a brief biography of each subject in the photo. Rationale: See above.

To protect your joy in this time of love and giving, do not use the ice-cube trays that make little ice golf balls for your holiday party drinks. They don't give a true roll and can cause significant damage when struck with a three iron. ■

Underwear's the safest bet.

The First Golfer

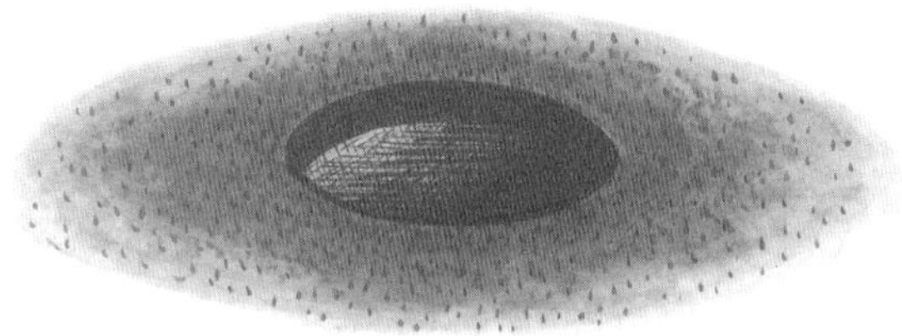

I'm not talking about some ancient Scotsman who invented the game thinking it might prove an amusing practical joke. Nor am I talking about the first pro in my life. (That happened to be my brother-in-law, who suggested I continue to play tennis.) The first golfer in your life is the first person who reveals, usually through his or her actions, the real meaning of the game.

I'm talking about Papa.

It hit all of us hard when Papa died. At 88 years old, his death was unexpected. That's because he lived a good portion of his life as a farmer in Red Springs, North Carolina, where many citizens live and play golf well into their 90s. Red Springs is also where my wife and my mother-in-law were born. (Papa was actually my grandfather-in-law.) It's an optimistic community; when these 90-plus-year-olds buy a new car, they opt for the extended warranty.

My wife took our family's grief and love to the funeral. I told our six-year-old twins that Papa was gone, then I went to look for solace myself. Since my pastor hadn't made the turn yet, I stopped in to see my pro. He was explaining to an older, well-dressed man (who looked like he could buy the golf course) why he didn't give senior-citizen discounts on his lessons. The older man closely resembled my father's image of the typical golfer. The image was not pretty. When the man began threatening to call in the AARP lawyers, I believe I may have saved my pro some serious legal fees by walking into, but not through, the glass door of the pro shop. Grief exhibits itself in singular ways. I told my pro I wanted to talk.

He listened.

I told him that my dad, who had owned a hardware and feed store in Illinois and whom I deeply loved, had been a tennis player. He'd said golf was a rich man's game and he didn't like rich men's games and I shouldn't either. So I didn't start playing golf until after my father died and I was seriously into my 40s.

Papa played to play, nothing more. There was always a wager, but it was the game that was important. Papa didn't drive around in a big car or wear fancy clothes. He loved his flower garden. He kept using the same balls over and over because his always landed in the fairway. His driving range was out behind the old boarding school near his house, and he shagged his own balls. The greens fees at his club were about $9. He was over 80 when I played with him there, and his biggest complaint was his loss of distance (although his ball still dropped onto the fairway and into the cup in several strokes less than mine).

He didn't look like an athlete, but he was. With his bald head, thin body and big ears, he looked like one of my father's good customers. If asked, Papa would tell you anything you wanted to know about your game, and he was always right, though he never offered anyone any unsolicited advice.

He grumbled at bogeys, did not comment on pars, and smiled at birdies. He completely destroyed the image my father had painted.

He grumbled at bogeys, did not comment on pars, and smiled at birdies. He completely destroyed the image my father had painted.

I thought of Dad and Papa. I wondered aloud if my life would have been different if the two of them had met. ■

Nine-its

I'd been having a significant case of nerves. It had nothing to do with all the bills that were piling up or the threats from the IRS or the fact that my six-year-old twins respond better to our parrot than to their infrequently home dad.

No, my problem was the front nine. I had "toppitis" on the tees, "grounditis" in the fairway, "flailitis" in the sand, and "yipitis" on the greens. The net result was a 50-plus-plus on the first nine holes. On the back nine, I was, according to my standards, reasonably flawless.

To counter my affliction I did what any serious golfer would do. I used part of the mortgage money to buy a new glove. My problem, obviously, was my tattered, stiff, smelly old golf glove. I bought a new one and called my pro.

It's Paulitis, I nervously laughed into the phone, the twitch in my shoulder almost under control.

"Still having trouble on the front nine?" he asked.

I forced myself to take a deep breath. I told him I was fine and that I had bought a new glove.

"Why don't you come over for lunch?" he asked.

An hour later, we were sit-

ting out on the clubhouse porch, eating burgers. We had burgers because my pro was buying. If I had been treating, it would have been a hot dog and chips. One meal I'd get the dog and my pro would get the chips. The next, we would switch.

"Let's talk about your kids," my pro said.

Kids? Kids? I paused. Then I remembered the twins. And the parrot. And my wife. And the mortgage. I started to twitch.

My pro ordered dessert for both of us.

Dessert? Look at the time! I had to meet my wife (what's her name?) in three hours! I had to catch a plane or train or something! I had to –!

"Would you look at that," he said, cutting into a huge piece of chocolate cake. He was watching some nearby golfers swallow hot dogs whole, tie their shoes on the run, and leap over hedges in a mad dash to the starter so they wouldn't lose their tee time. Everything looked normal to me.

My pro ordered a second glass of iced tea. He began telling me about the time he'd caddied at the Masters and how sensational it was.

I looked at my watch. I needed to hit that ball.

"Did you see the tournament last Saturday?" he asked, clinking the ice in his glass.

Well, yes, I replied. We started to talk about it. We talked about the twins (what were their names?) and how anxious they were to learn to play golf. We talked about his son and daughter. Proud fathers, us. I ordered a second glass of iced tea.

"You ready?" he asked after we'd shared a few funny stories about our old home towns.

Ready for what?

He nodded his head toward the tee box.

As we teed up, my pro kept up a light chatter about the problems he'd encountered when he'd first taken up the game. No other golfers were in sight; the pack had launched their attack – shoe laces dangling, mustard dripping from their chins – more than an hour before.

The first ball strangely sailed over 220 yards down the fairway. I say "strangely" because I was the one who had hit it. My pro's ball bested the one already out there (mine, I had to remind myself) by a good 25 yards.

As we approached my Titleist, I pulled out what I considered to be the appropriate iron, and I knocked the ball somewhat short of the pin but out of any danger. My pro's ball landed four feet from the cup.

Pulling up to the second hole, I was laughing so hard at a joke he had told me – guy's wife tells him how incredibly lucky he is to keep finding tees under his ball in the fairway – my spikes caught the side of the cart and I fell to my knees. The fact that my pro had just marked down his birdie and a four in my box didn't even phase me.

The rest of the afternoon was fun. I got some fives and sixes, a couple more fours. I heard the birds singing. I saw two young deer at the edge of the woods, waiting for us to pass. I almost sank a 10-foot putt.

I remembered my wife's name, remembered that the reason I enjoyed being out on the links was because of the peace and quiet and beauty. I remembered how smart my pro was.

I also remembered the new glove I'd left on the front seat of my car. ■

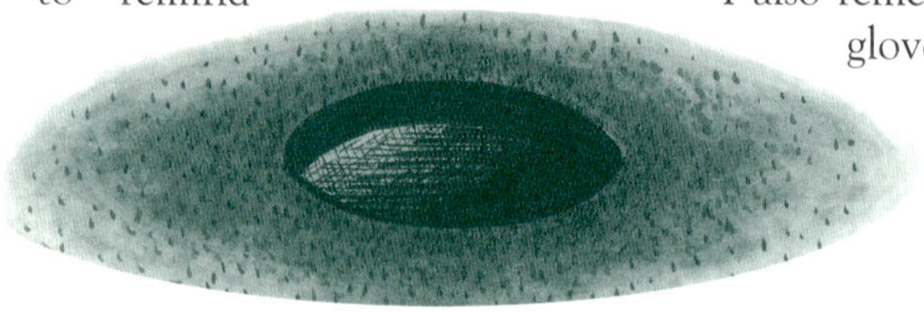

About the Author

Paul deVere is a syndicated columnist, freelance journalist, scriptwriter, television producer, advertising consultant, lecturer and self-proclaimed novice golfer whose novitiate continues unabated. His articles on golf and other topics appear in regional newspapers and various national magazines (golf-related and others). A graduate of Loras College, Dubuque, Iowa, he has attempted to avoid writing by being an actor, goatherd, teacher and advertising executive. All attempts have failed. He lives, plays golf and writes on Hilton Head Island, South Carolina, with his wife, two children, two dogs, cat, rabbit, fish and birds.

About the Illustrator

Ashley Holt, professional illustrator and 1996 graduate of Savannah College of Art and Design, lives in Savannah, Georgia.

If You Think THIS Book Is Funny ...

Saron Press, Ltd., publishes and distributes a variety of unique golf-related books, audio tapes, calendars and T-shirts (including ones bearing designs appearing in this book). Quantity discounts and wholesale pricing available. For further information, please contact:

Nora Coleman
SARON PRESS, LTD.
Box 4990
Hilton Head Island, South Carolina 29938
VOICE 803.363.6697/FAX 803.363.6698